Ian Thorpe

W.M. Anderson

CAMBRIDGE UNIVERSITY PRESS

PUBLISHED BY THE PRESS SYNDICATE OF THE UNIVERSITY OF CAMBRIDGE
The Pitt Building, Trumpington Street, Cambridge, United Kingdom

CAMBRIDGE UNIVERSITY PRESS
The Edinburgh Building, Cambridge CB2 2RU, UK
40 West 20th Street, New York, NY 10011–4211, USA
477 Williamstown Road, Port Melbourne 3207, Australia
Ruiz de Alarcón 13, 28014 Madrid, Spain
Dock House, The Waterfront, Cape Town 8001, South Africa

http://www.cambridge.edu.au

© Cambridge University Press 2002

Notice to teachers
It is illegal to reproduce any part of this work in material form (including photocopying and electronic storage)
except under the following circumstances:
(i) where you are abiding by a licence granted to your school or institution by the Copyright Agency Limited that permits the copying of small parts of text, in limited quantities, within the conditions set out in the licence;
(ii) where no such licence exists, or where you wish to exceed the terms of the licence, and you have gained the written permission of Cambridge University Press.

First published in 2002

Edited by Judith Simpson
Typeset by J&M Typesetting
Printed in Australia by Hyde Park Press, South Australia

Typeface Palatino 14/16 pt. *System* QuarkXPress® [MK]

National Library of Australia Cataloguing in Publication data
   Anderson, Wendy.
   Livewire Australian celebrities: Ian Thorpe.
   ISBN 0 521 52673 6.
   1. Thorpe, Ian, 1982– . 2. Swimmers — Australia — Biography. I. Title. II. Title: Australian celebrities: Ian Thorpe. (Series: Livewire series).
   797.21092

ISBN 0 521 52673 6 paperback

Acknowledgements
Photographs: AAP Image for pp. iv (by Julian Smith) and 10 (by Darrin Braybrook); ALLSPORT for p. 25; News Ltd for cover and pp. 4, 12, 16, 19 and 22.

Every effort has been made to trace and acknowledge copyright but there may be instances where this has not been possible. Cambridge University Press would welcome any information that would redress this situation.

Contents

		Page
1	I'm Bored!	1
2	Home Life	3
3	Getting Wet	6
4	Clever Too	7
5	Record Maker	9
6	Just for Fun	15
7	A Proud Australian	18
8	A Famous Face	20
9	Famous Feet	21
10	The Thorpedo!	26

Ian and American swimmer, Amanda Beard, at the 2001 Telstra awards in Melbourne. Ian became Telstra Australian Swimmer of the Year for the third year running.

1 I'm Bored!

Christina is training.
She is swimming up and down
and up and down.

Christina is a distance swimmer.

A little boy is sitting by the pool.
He is watching her.

Christina does a tumble turn.
She wants to swim for Australia.

Right now, she is at
Padstow Swimming Club in Sydney.

The boy swings his feet.
He is bored.

This boy is allergic to chlorine.
When he is in the pool,
he has to wear a nose plug.

He does belly flops.
He has to swim with
his head out of the water.

The boy has a weak chest too.
He gets coughs.

But he is sick of having
to watch his big sister train.

He looks around.
There's nothing for him to do —
just swimming.

He might as well give it a go.
It will help pass the time
while Christina trains.

Little do they know,
the boy will become
a legend in the pool.

Christina makes it to
the Australian swim squad.
But shoulder problems mean
that she will have to stop swimming.

She will go on
to help manage
her brother's career.

Christina's bored little brother
is Ian Thorpe.

2 Home Life

Ian James Thorpe was born in Sydney
on 13 October 1982.

His dad, Ken, worked as a gardener.
Ken loves to be outdoors.
He plays golf to relax.
He also loves cricket.
But he cannot swim!

Ken's father, Ian's grandfather,
was very keen on cricket.
He pushed Ken to be good at it.

Ken made up his mind
never to push his own children.

Christina and Ian chose to swim.
They swam because they liked it.

Ian still says,
'My aims as a swimmer
have always been simple —
to enjoy what I do
and to get the best out of myself'.

4 March 1999: Ian and his mum, Margaret, at Sydney Town Hall where Ian was presented with *The Daily Telegraph* New South Wales Sports Star of the Year award.

Home is a safe place for Ian.
The Thorpes are a very close family.

Ian says his mum and dad
are his biggest fans.
They watch every time he races.

Ian's mother's name is Margaret.
She is a teacher.

She is also a great cook.
Ian loves home-cooked roasts.

Like most mothers,
Margaret worries about her son.

She makes sure Ian eats
all the healthy food
a champion athlete needs.

And Ian says her best advice is,
'Never forget who you are
or where you come from'.

3 Getting Wet

Ian has a gift for swimming.
He swam in his first competition
when he was about eight.

Ian went to Milperra Public School.
Then he went to
East Hills Boys Technical High.
These schools are in Sydney.

He grew out of
his allergy to chlorine —
luckily for him!

In his early days,
Ian swam different strokes
and different distances.

He swam backstroke, breaststroke
and butterfly,
as well as freestyle.
And he was good at all of them.

In 1996,
Ian won nine gold medals
at the National Junior Championships!

4 Clever Too

Ian was a good student.
He got high marks at school.
Maths was his worst subject.

He left school in Year 10.
It was time to train for
the Sydney 2000 Olympics Games.

He had to finish
his Year 10 lessons by mail.
He could do this at any time
or any place.

Training is very hard.
Ian wakes up at 4.15 am.
He swims for more than two hours.

Then he has to do some
weight training in the gym.
He does some boxing too.

At 3.30 in the afternoon
he goes back to the pool for
two or three more hours of swimming!

Imagine doing all of that
and your schoolwork too!

Ian likes to keep his brain busy.
He is learning French.

Ian hopes to finish Year 12.
He thinks that
he would like to be a doctor.

He likes to read too.
The Power of One by Bryce Courtenay
is one of Ian's favourite books.

That is not a surprise.
It is about a clever and caring boy.
He becomes a champion at his sport.
Now who does that sound like?

5 Record Maker

Ian has set many records for swimming.
He has broken lots of records too.

At the Pan Pacific trials in 1997,
Ian broke six national records.

He is the youngest male swimmer
to be in an Australian team.
That was in 1997 too.
Ian was 14 years old.

Ian is also the youngest male
to swim for Australia.

Before that, John Konrads
had the record.
Konrads was 15 when he was picked
for the 1956 Melbourne Olympics.
But Konrads was not able to swim
in that Olympic team.

Ian won gold in
his first international swim!
It was the 400-metre freestyle.
He beat his friend Grant Hackett.

Ian talks to his coach, Doug Frost, during training for the 1998 Commonwealth Games in Kuala Lumpur, Malaysia.

In 1998, Ian became
the youngest male World Champion.
He also won four gold medals at
the Commonwealth Games.

At the 1999 Pan Pacific Championships
he broke four world records in four days.
It was in Sydney.

Ian says the 400-metre freestyle win
was the best.
It was his first
long-course world record.

Ian broke the record
held by fellow Australian,
Kieren Perkins.

Kieren was one of Ian's heroes.
Ian sent a Hero Fax to Kieren
at the 1992 Barcelona Olympic Games.
Ian was nine years old.

Now kids send Hero Faxes to Ian!

Ian concentrates on beating his own times when he is swimming. Here he is training before the start of the 2001 Goodwill Games in Brisbane.

Ian never thinks about
the people he is racing.
He does not aim to beat others.
He races against himself.
He aims to beat his own times.

Until the Sydney 2000 Olympics,
the Americans had never lost the
men's 4 × 100-metre freestyle relay.

Ian was part of the amazing team
that beat them.
It was an exciting race.

Ian says,
'I would take that win over anything
I have achieved in my career'.
He loves being part of a team.

He was also a member of
the world-record-breaking
4 × 200-metre freestyle relay team.

Ian ended the 2000 Olympic Games
with three gold medals
and two silver medals.

At the 2001 World Championships
at Fukuoka in Japan,
Ian won six gold medals.
He is the first man to win so many.

He set new world records
for the 400-metre freestyle on 22 July,
for the 800-metre freestyle on 24 July
and for the 200-metre freestyle on 25 July.

On 27 July, with team-mates
Grant Hackett, Michael Klim
and William Kirby, Ian also set
a new world's best time
for the 4 × 200-metre freestyle relay.

What a legend!

6 Just for Fun

Like most of us,
Ian watches television to relax.
He enjoys comedies.
He likes *Ally McBeal* and *Friends*.

Now that he is famous,
Ian gets to do some exciting things.

He was on his favourite TV show.
He sat in Central Perk Cafe on *Friends*
and drank coffee in the background.
Right behind all the stars!

He loves movies too.
Adam Sandler films make him laugh.
Billy Madison is his favourite.

Ian also likes action movies like
Traffic with Michael Douglas
and *The Long Kiss Goodnight*.
He says that is an all-time favourite.

And guess what?
He met one of the stars of that too!
Geena Davis came to Sydney
for the Olympics.
Ian chatted with her then.

Ian often takes part in fundraising events. 'America Beanie Baby', signed by Ian, was auctioned to raise money for the Australian victims of the 11 September 2001 terrorist attacks.

Ian is invited to awesome places.
He wore a white suit to the opening of
the Fox Studios in Sydney.

When *Mission Impossible 2* opened,
Ian met Tom Cruise and Nicole Kidman.
He was surprised that
they had so much respect for him.

Fashion designer Giorgio Armani
invited Ian to New York.
Ian had a great time.
He loves shopping for clothes.

In America he went to watch
Jay Leno's Tonight Show.
Instead of just watching,
Ian got to be on the show.

But not all of Ian's life is like this.
He is happy just to be at home.
He plays computer games
and listens to CDs.

Ian enjoys all kinds of music.
Greenday, Offspring, Blink 182
and Destiny's Child are bands he likes.

Going to the beach with his mates
is Ian's idea of a fun day —
more swimming!

7 A Proud Australian

People have been watching Ian
since he was very young.
He had to grow up quickly.

He always sets a good example.
He speaks and behaves well
and is a modest person.

In 1999, Ian was given
the Sir Donald Bradman Award.

This award is 'for the athlete who,
through their example in sport,
has most inspired Australia'.

This award means more to Ian
than being Swimmer of the Year.

In 2000, Ian was
Young Australian of the Year.
He says it was a great honour.

Ian is proud to be Australian
and Australia is proud of Ian Thorpe!

Ian swims with the sharks at Sydney Aquarium to launch his Omega watch.

8 A Famous Face

Ian is a swimming superstar.
He has many sponsors.
He has become rich.

He advertises many products.
His face is known all over the world.

Ian is especially popular in Japan.
He starred in an advertisement
for Coca-Cola there.

He was also chosen for some
anti-drugs advertisements in Japan.
The message was 'No. Never.'

Even young people in Japan
admire Ian.

Ian has a famous face.
Sometimes this is hard.

People always notice Ian.
He does not get much privacy.

9 Famous Feet

Ian's feet are famous too.

He has very big feet.
They are size 17.

Some people call him Flipper.
Some even think that his feet
make him a great swimmer.
But it takes much more
than big feet
to be a champion swimmer.

Ian is a big man.
He is 195 centimetres tall.

His arm span is
about 190 centimetres.
That means he has
an incredibly long stroke.

Being strong is important too.
Ian is all muscle.
He has very low body fat.

Ian shows off his famous feet and one of his many medals! The medal is for winning the 400-metre freestyle race at the 8th World Swimming Championships in Perth on 16 January 1998.

Ian is also extremely flexible.
He bends easily.
This is a plus for athletes.

Ian swims very high on the water.
This helps make him faster.

Alexandre Popov was a legend
in 100-metre freestyle.
He is one of Ian's sporting heroes.

Popov was famous for his six-beat kick.
Ian uses the same type of kick.

Have you ever used a kickboard?
Do you feel as if you kick and kick
but hardly move?

Not Ian!
He can move a kickboard
almost as fast as he can swim.

Ian needs a big kick.
It goes with his big stroke.

But that big kick makes waves.
It chops up the water behind Ian.

This makes it harder for swimmers
in the lanes next to him.

It's hard to swim fast
if the water is not smooth.

One swimmer said that
swimming behind Ian was like
being in a washing machine!

Some swimmers try not to be
in the lanes near Ian
for the actual races.

They have to time their heats
extra carefully.
They worry about it.
This gives Ian a mental advantage.

Ian is a winner for lots of reasons.
Don't forget his winning attitude.

But those big bendy feet do help.

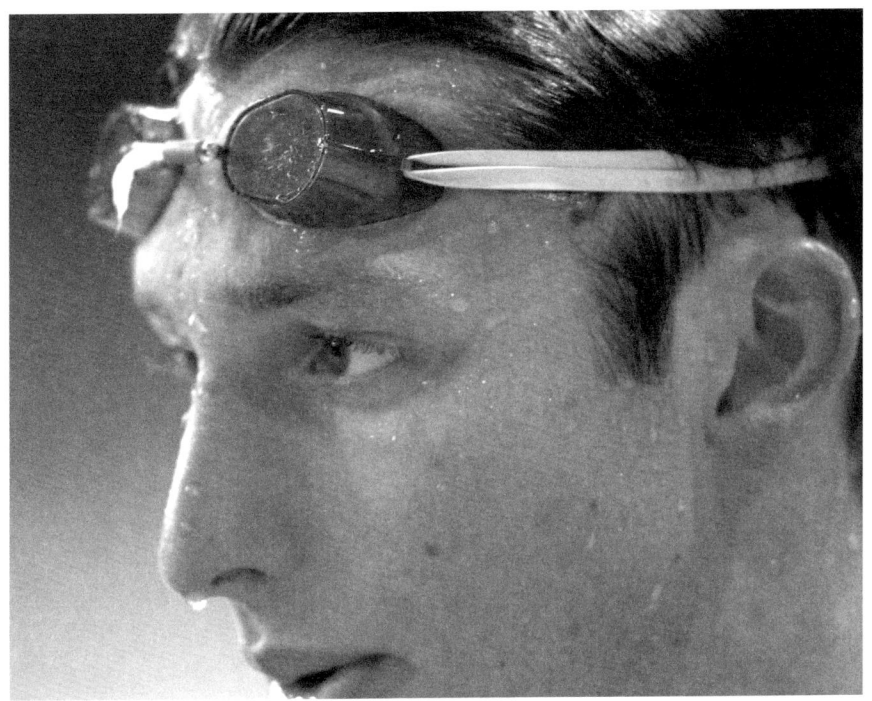

Staying focused under pressure is a part of Ian's winning attitude.

10 The Thorpedo!

So is Ian Thorpe the perfect athlete?
Is there anything Ian can't do?

You may remember
that Ian's dad was a good cricketer.
Ken Thorpe played for Bankstown.
So did Mark and Steve Waugh!

Well, Ian has a problem with cricket.
He cannot hit the ball!

Ian did play other sports
when he was very young
but he is not good at ball sports.

He gave up other sports
when he was about 12 years old.
He chose to focus on swimming.

Until his seventeenth birthday,
Ian used to run for training.

That day in 1999 Ian was running
through Royal National Park.
He rolled his ankle on a rock.
It hurt but he kept going.

After swim training,
Ian went for an x-ray.
His ankle was broken.

He was out of the water for four days.
Then he continued his training.

Can you imagine swimming with
a fibreglass cast on your foot?
For six hours a day!

That's what Ian did.

Ian enjoys the daily grind
of lap training.
He says, 'I love doing what I do
more than anything else'.

He is looking forward to more
swimming meets all over the world.
He has his sights set on doing well
at the Olympic Games in Athens in 2004.

He says he doesn't know how far
he can go in swimming.
'I don't yet know where the line is,
but when I find it,
I hope I can jump over it.'

Ian Thorpe is an amazing athlete.
He is an amazing person.

Strong of body and mind.
Fast.
That's the Thorpedo!

CARMEL COLLEGE
PRESCOT ROAD
ST. HELENS
MERSEYSIDE
WA10 3AG